HOW TO WIN AN ELECTION

A HANDBOOK FOR THE CITIZEN POLITICIAN

CHARLES MOSCOWITZ

TABLE OF CONTENTS

1

WINNING

I ran for Congress in the 4th congressional district of Massachusetts in 2004 against Rep. Barney Frank. At the time I was a local radio talk show host, an author and a small business owner who had never run for political office before. While I lost the race, I nevertheless raised a half a million dollars, I received wide media coverage in Massachusetts, and I debated the sitting congressman a half a dozen times both in debates and on TV. For me the experience was both exhilarating and devastating. I now feel compelled, 15 years later and in the aftermath of the highly contested 2020 election loss of President Donald Trump to Joe Biden, to share my thoughts and my experiences as a matter of civic duty.

While I write this short treatise as a Trump supporter and as a Republican, nevertheless, the issues that I cover here may apply to any potential citizen candidate from any party or political perspective. While my goal is to encourage Republicans and conservatives to run for office, I nevertheless contend that any registered voter should consider running. If you are a housewife or a house husband, or if you are unemployed, or retired, or an empty-nester, or a teenager, or if you simply have time on your hands you should consider running for office. If you run based on an issue or two that you are passionate about, and your issues are relevant to the office that you seek, you will be heard. Whether or not you win, the media will allow you, one way or another, to raise your issues. You might be surprised to learn how many of your fellow citizens care about the same issues you care about and, thanks to you and to your candidacy, those issues will enter into public consciousness and will be injected into public discourse. While this might sound like a cliche, you can make a difference.

You certainly can win, especially if you are running for local office. You might be surprised to learn that your local elected School Committee member, Comptroller, Registrar of Deeds, City Councilor, Alderman, Town Meeting member, Mayor, City or State Committeemen, State Representative, State Senator or the holder of any other various local offices has been in office for a long time and has possibly served unopposed for several terms. Indeed, such an incumbent is likely acting in a fairly low-key manner and has, as such, gotten used to resting on his or her laurels. It is relatively easy for you to look into the voting record of the incumbent as most of that information is part of a public record that has most likely gone unexamined and unnoticed.

You might get lucky and discover a few bombshells within that record, bombshells that are fair game in a political campaign. Your research might, in this regard, yield low-hanging fruit that is there for the pickin. You might discover that a longtime incumbent might have fallen into certain careless habits such as not showing up to meetings and public events, not casting votes or, worse, offering favors and patronage to unqualified family members and friends. In this regard, look for the quid pro quo, or I scratch your back, you scratch mine. You might get lucky and discover that the office holder does not actually live in the district or that they might be tax delinquent or might be involved in some other misdemeanor or worse. While all of this is fair political fodder, you should be careful when releasing this type of information. Traditional experienced politicians, rather than getting their own hands dirty, will often turn to surrogates and, once the cat is out of the bag, the politician is then free to stride in and take it up.

Before running, you might want to conduct research on yourself and create your own private dossier to determine what, if anything, might be raised about you of a negative nature by your opponent and by the media. Be prepared to answer negative information that might emerge about you and practice your responses in advance. As the old saying goes, politics is not bean-bag. Late 19th Century American philosopher Henry Adams observed: *Politics, as a practice, whatever its professions, has always been the systematic organization of hatreds.* (1.) Before getting into the game, even at the local level, you might consider evaluating whether or not your involvement might negatively impact you professionally or personally. When contemplating a run, you ought to consider the best interests of your family and how your candidacy might negatively impact your standing in your community.

It would be your most basic function as a candidate to stand up tall and articulate a couple of positive issues while at the same time contrasting those issues favorably to those of your opponent. You will need to articulate, in clear, concise and easy to understand terms who you are, what you believe in and why you are running. You will need to do a deep dive into the select issues that you choose to champion while keeping abreast of any and all generally relevant news developments affecting your district including issues that might seem trivial on the surface. The best way to do this, besides reading any news you can get your hands on, is to develop a network of friends and supporters who keep their ear to the ground and who check in with you regularly. Knowing your district, its people, its history, its economy, its culture, its problems, will prove to be your greatest currency and will be the biggest factor in terms of your standing out from the pack. Your command of such knowledge, when articulated by you, is what people will remember most about you when they go to the polls and vote.

This book is not meant for hacks and insiders. Such candidates have few if any principles or scruples and they usually do not have much of a discernable internal moral structure. They are careerists who seek office strictly out of ambition and to fuel their overweening and misplaced narcissism. We should remember that positions of power are always coveted by those who seek power as an end in and of itself and for personal glory which they learn to disguise, sometimes even to themselves. Indeed, this type of candidate makes up, and has always made up, the majority of those who seek and who hold office. While it should be acknowledged that ambition and vanity serve as an inevitable and corrupting element within anyone who seeks office, this book seeks to reach the average working citizen who holds the rare quality of placing principle above ambition.

Legends abound regarding the late great US Speaker of the House, Thomas P. "Tip" O'Neill Jr. of Massachusetts who was known as the consummate politician in his day. Tip was most strongly associated with the aphorism *All Politics is Local*. Two legends regarding Tip O'Neill are worth recalling for the purpose of this book. After Tip lost his first race for Cambridge City Council, *a neighbor told him that she would vote for him, "even though you didn't ask me." When O'Neill protested that he had known her since he was a child, had shoveled her walk and cut her grass, and didn't think he had to ask for her vote, she replied, "Tom, let me tell you something. People like to be asked."*(2.)

This gets to the simplest most urgent and most fundamental principle of winning at politics. The candidate has got to ask his constituents to vote for him or her. He must preferably ask directly and in person and the request is best done with a look in the eye and a handshake. Other vehicles for this appeal include the phone call, which is second best, as well as appeals by advertisements, letters and social media. The winning politician asks as many of his constituents as possible for their vote, including his closest friends and his associates, even including his own spouse, his own brother and his own mother. This simple act forces the candidate out of his comfort zone. It is natural not to ask another person to do something especially when the person being asked is a total stranger. The candidate must get over this natural reluctance to ask for something and he must ask if he expects to win.

The successful candidate must exude an air of confidence and he or she must develop a swagger that sets him or her apart. You are asking the voter to place you in a position of leadership, to make you their leader and, as such, you must act, and you must look like a leader. George Washington set the tone for how the American leader should look and act. Washington was acutely aware that as the first president of the USA his appearance and his actions would serve as an example to be emulated going forward. Washington cared about how he was addressed, how he entered the room, how he looked when he was mounted on his horse, his clothes, how his hair was combed, how he spoke and how he was spoken to. A politician, for example, should try not to attend a meeting or enter a room unaccompanied. Examples of politicians today who developed a distinctive look and style would include Hillary Clinton, Donald Trump, Elizabeth Warren and Bernie Sanders.

The winning candidate must also learn how to ask his constituents for money, he or she must do what is called in political parlance "dialing for dollars." Every successful candidate and every successful office holder, without exception, learns how to do this unpleasant and at times draining task. Congressmen and Senators regularly trek over to buildings that were set up near the US Capitol by both the Democratic and the Republican parties as fundraising centers in order to make fundraising calls. No doubt, Presidents Barack Obama and Donald Trump made fundraising calls and probably did so from the Oval Office. No candidate wins and no office holder survives unless they learn how to do this as part of their regular routine.

The other important principle emanating from the legendary career of Tip O'Neill that we might consider is that he gathered signatures for his state house run by going door to door in his district. This was no small feat for Tip who was obese and who was known to be a heavy drinker. According to legend, Tip spent months knocking on doors every weekday evening where he met thousands of voters. The experience transformed him both politically and personally as he had the opportunity to hear directly from thousands of people. He heard their stories, he heard what they were going through and he learned how to interact with strangers. The experience changed both his political opinions and his life. (3.)

I believe that Donald Trump experienced something similar as a result of his running for president and meeting and talking with thousands of people face to face, people who he would not have otherwise had the opportunity to have met. When the Access Hollywood scandal broke late in his presidential campaign, a scandal in which a private taped conversation between him and TV host Billy Bush was released to the public, a conversation where he had made lewd and disgusting comments about women, he responded by first taking responsibility and noting his embarrassment and by then claiming that he had changed since the time of the conversation which had taken place several years previous. Trump claimed that he had changed as a result of his having met and talked with thousands of people during his campaign.

I believe Donald Trump on this claim because I experienced this same phenomena myself during my own campaign in 2004. During that campaign I personally gathered well over a thousand signatures from voters by going door to door, by standing in front of supermarkets, by standing outside of train and subway stations and by working the crowd at events like the Boston Marathon. While I was met with both friendship and hostility, many of the people that I met had opinions on politics and they wanted to engage with me and debate with me. Much of my thinking before then had emanated from books and from talking to political thinkers and intellectuals on my radio program. The experience of getting out there on the street and hearing the real experiences and concerns of real people dealing with real problems transformed me, brought me from the theoretical to the real, and in many ways, modified my opinions and my positions on many issues.

And, so, I encourage you to run for political office both as a civic responsibility and as an experience that will enrich your life. You can contribute something positive to society and to your country by promoting ideas to your fellow citizens while finding purpose in life and, if you win, by serving. I hope to contribute toward the development of an army of American citizen candidates who take on the elitist class of politically connected professional hack politicians.

History provides an example of such civic virtue in the Roman farmer Lucius Quintus Cincinnatus who was called upon by his countrymen to leave his farm and serve as dictator in response to an emergency. Cincinnatus served just long enough to deal with the emergency after which he returned to his farm. George Washington, likewise, refused to run for a third term as president choosing instead to return to his farm at Mount Vernon.

DEMOCRACY

Democracy does not grow on trees. We do not wake up every morning, pour ourselves a cup of hot coffee, look out our kitchen window and see democracy growing out of the ground. As Americans, we tend to take democracy for granted as we have all been privileged enough to not experience life in a war zone or under the jack-boot of a communist dictator. For this reason, it is more difficult for us to comprehend or to even imagine the fact that democracy does not exist in nature and, as such, that democracy is a fragile thing that can atrophy and die if it is not exercised with regularity.

I suggest that the events of the year 2020, the pandemic, the turbulent election, might offer us a glimpse into the fragility and precariousness of our democracy and why it is important for every citizen, each in his own way, to contribute in some way toward preserving and advancing the democratic freedoms that we take for granted. Before we proceed with a brief exposition of the events of 2020, and what we might derive politically from those events, please allow me to present a short primer on democracy itself, what democracy is and what democracy means.

Let me start by noting that the United States of America is not a democracy per se, but, rather, that the USA is a federated Republic of States established on a written constitution that recognizes democratic principles. As the Pledge of Allegiance states: *To the Republic for which we stand*. The founding generation viewed democracy as mob rule, or majority rule, which is why they established a limited government *of laws and not of men* as stated by John Adams and, as such, a government that protects the inalienable rights of the minority over the mob tendencies that are inherent with majority rule. The American system is one that constitutes an indirect democracy, one that diffuses and balances political power between several branches of government at several levels. The founding generation accurately understood government as a legalized and, as such, as a dangerous form of force. This was why they

13

devised a system of divided and competing
political entities, each with its own assigned
mission, and each keeping the others honest in a
perpetual state of checks and balances.

Our political system is based upon a devolution
of governing powers, a system of political
subsidiarity by which local government is the most
powerful. Indeed, the most local form of
government, the school board, the planning board,
the town meeting, the city council, the county
Sheriff and government, the Mayor, was
traditionally the most powerful form of government
because local government had the most impact on
the lives of the citizen. The local elected school
board member, for example, would likely have a
child in the public school system and would be a
neighbor who could be approached. The local
elected official has the most real-life knowledge
regarding the conditions of the community they
were elected to represent, and they are the most
accountable to the community where they live. The
local elected Sheriff, for example, is traditionally
the highest law enforcement official in America.

The three-tiered system of checks and balances,
as enshrined within the US Constitution and as
emulated by the respective State Constitutions, is
more complex than that which is formally

recognized. The balance of power extends to the balance between the Federal Government and the States and, within the States, between the State Government, the counties and the local municipality. The Amendments to the US Constitution recognize the balance between the Federal Government and the sovereign citizen as would be the case, for example, regarding the Second Amendment right to keep and bear arms which is juxtaposed and balanced by the right of the state and the local municipality to recognize a well-regulated militia. This concept is amplified by the Ninth and Tenth Amendments to the US Constitution which recognizes that all governing powers not specifically assigned by the US Constitution to the Federal Government reside with the States and with the ultimate sovereign, the people under God who is recognized by the Declaration of Independence as the source of all sovereignty. Indeed, the concept of a balance of powers into a three-tier system exists in nature, it exists in the everyday life of the individual and it exists in Christianity in the form of the Trinity.

Thus, the concept of the balance of power, in its various manifestations, and the concept of subsidiarity, by which local government holds the most governing responsibility, are the concepts that define the American political philosophy of indirect democracy. The underlying principle of this philosophy holds that by balancing and, as such, by diffusing governmental powers, the maximum powers reside at its source of power, which is with the citizen, under God, who, as Thomas Jefferson noted in the Declaration of Independence, endows us with certain unalienable rights, among these, life, liberty and the pursuit of happiness. It is our responsibility as citizens to remember to exercise the levers of that democracy in order to keep it balanced and functioning smoothly for ourselves and our posterity.

Events of the year 2020 demonstrate that we as citizens, and our local elected officials in many cases, have forgotten how to exercise those sovereign powers or even that we hold those powers in the first place. The seizure of governmental powers by State Governors responding to the real health crisis of the Covid 19 pandemic, the arbitrary mandates of mask wearing, the shutdown of businesses and other often arbitrary rules, often without the consent of state legislatures and local municipalities, represents a serious break from the balance of power principle, not to mention the rule of law and this launched a trend, I would argue, toward authoritarianism. While perhaps many if not most of those regulations may have been in order, although this is debatable, the political system itself was abrogated under the guise of the emergency and this set-in motion a dangerous transfer of governing powers from the sovereign citizen and their elected representative to the executive.

A second development of 2020 that constitutes a breach of our political system of checks and balances pertains to governmental excess in terms of election regulations. Article Two of the US Constitution states that the state legislature exercises the sole authority to regulate elections and that includes all elections, state and federal, including the election for president which is, de facto, fifty state elections held simultaneously. Under the guise of the Covid 19 emergency, in 2020, state governors, state secretaries of states and state courts usurped those constitutional powers from the state legislatures. These usurpations included such practices, which were issued as decrees by governors and by secretaries of states and without the benefit of public debate, hearings, or a vote by the peoples courts, which is what state legislatures are, as mass unsolicited mailings of ballots, changes in rules pertaining to absentee voting, ballot harvesting, drop-boxes, and extending the election day beyond the first Tuesday in November as stipulated by the US Constitution.

In Pennsylvania, for example, such changes to election laws by the governor were challenged by the state legislature which appealed to the state Supreme Court which turned the legislature down. The challenge eventually made its way to the Supreme Court which ultimately refused to hear the case in spite of the fact that the law regarding elections was not in dispute but is, rather, in the US Constitution in clear and unambiguous language. More recently, a state judge in Michigan, in response to a lawsuit brought by a state representative, struck down a decree that had been enacted by Michigan Secretary of State Jocelyn Benson, a decree that changed the law pertaining to signature verification for absentee ballots. Benson ruled that the voter signature on the absentee ballot, going forward, would only have to possess a vague similarity to the voter signature on file at the clerk's office.

One of the positive lessons emerging from the year 2020 is that state legislatures and local governments have a lot more authority than had been previously assumed. The political trend, one which began to accelerate in the early part of the 20th Century, particularly with the election of Woodrow Wilson as president in 1912, has been the gradual transfer of governing powers from local elected officials to the national government and private entities. That year witnessed the passage of the 16th Amendment which allowed the Federal Government to directly tax individual income. and which also allowed for the creation of non-profits and foundations which would, over subsequent centuries, come to dominate our culture. These entities would become a revolving door between government and elite monied interests and would further centralize the public-private partnership that has replaced local elected government. This process further accelerated under the Franklin D. Roosevelt administration as FDR, under the guise of the emergency of the depression, assumed emergency powers and established a plethora of federal agencies, known as the alphabet agencies, which would themselves assume sovereign powers that had previously been exercised by elected officials, by the states and by the people.

Those times witnessed the development of a parallel accelerating trend which involved the transfer of government powers, those which were supposed to be held by elected representatives of the people, to semi-private sovereign and in many cases self-regulated agencies, unaccountable agencies made up of faceless bureaucrats making laws by other names. The trend became international after World War II when, in the guise of promoting world peace, the United Nations, the

World Trade Organization, the International Monetary Fund, UNESCO, and a plethora of Non-Governmental Organizations began to consolidate governing powers on a global scale. These trends, along with economic and cultural globalization, diminished the powers of local government.

Now is the time for the American citizen politician, the working person who is concerned with local issues and who believes in freedom and democratic principles, to reassert control over the rightful levers of power, to take those powers back from the corrupted political ruling class both elected and unelected. These natural powers lay dormant, and they are waiting to be tapped by citizen politicians who are "woke" in the real sense of the word. It is now well past time for we, the people, to re-assert our American birthright of self-government both for ourselves and our posterity.

THE MEDIA

Whether you love or whether you hate Donald Trump, and I happen to love Trump, He undeniably changed the cultural landscape of American politics in terms of how our political leaders communicate. He changed both the mechanics and the style of political communication in a way that opens up the democratic process for the citizen politician and for this, I would suggest, both his anti-establishment supporters and his anti-establishment detractors owe him a debt of gratitude. Donald Trump, by force of his own at times garrulous and ribald personality, blew a gaping hole into the media elite control over the means of communication and by doing so he essentially swung the door of opportunity open to the citizen politician.

The ruling elites, those who have dominated our institutions of politics, academia, the media, big corporations, our cultural and religious institutions, are accustomed to communicating in a style that was described by French scholar and historian Alain Besancon and the language of totalitarianism. (4.) They speak and they write in a pseudo-intellectual cant, often assuming slight phony British accents as they effect a gangrenous jargon that is indirect, sophistic, and is often impenetrable as they operate in a rarefied universe involving code-words, double-speak, submerged meanings and elaborate, subtle, and labyrinthine webs of falsehoods and lies that are couched and subsumed within deeper layers of lies.

They either pick up on this style at an early age or they learn it in the finishing schools that are a major component of what we call Colleges. The ruling elitist is only slightly conscious of the fact that he engages in this type of discourse which he more often employs when speaking in public. The skilled practitioner of this type of cant is often able to seamlessly express two or more contradictory opinions in the same sentence. In a nut-shell, he or she knows how to either say nothing, and to do so gloriously, or he or she intrinsically knows how to lie without a trace, a type of lying that he or she is not necessarily conscious of. This style of communication is the hallmark of a ruling class that has no real moral conviction and, more fundamentally, the individual practitioner has only a vague sense of who he or she is.

Like the biblical Abraham smashing the idols in his father, Trump burst onto the scene smashing idols. In this way, by his use of language, Trump not only threatened the assumed power of the elite, but he threatened the tenuous and personal grip that many elitists hold on reality itself. So where, then, does that put the citizen candidate who, whether or not this is acknowledged, is now operating in Trump's footsteps in this regard? In a nut-shell, the citizen candidate is now free to speak in plain, unadorned and unvarnished language. The candidate no longer needs to worry about every single word that he says but he or she is now free to speak out with calm, careful confidence and self-awareness. This does not mean the candidate should emulate Trump's propensity for crude and rude remarks as, in fact, the candidate should not emulate that part of Trump's character which did not serve him well. This simply means that the candidate needs not fear plain talk. The candidate does not have to weigh every word and he does not have to put on airs and come off like a phony priggish elitist jackass.

Expect the elite, acting either directly or acting through one of their local unconscious proxy surrogates, to try to shoot you down and to try to trip you up. The weapon du jour is to call you a racist, sexist, homophobe, or some other such similar epithet. As a non-conforming candidate, you run the risk of being on the receiving end of these hateful and ugly charges and, interestingly, it does not matter whether you happen to be black or a person of color, or whether you happen to be a woman or whether you are gay. In fact, if you happen to fall into any of these identities, you might expect an attack against you of this nature to be even more ferocious and vicious than if you were a white man as your candidacy may be perceived by them as an even greater threat to their identity narrative and their agit-prop.

You must not blink for one second when they start to throw this kind of mud at you and that is not easy to do because this kind of slander is damaging, and it hurts. Your ability to stand up and say no to this will be a mark of your metal and a proving ground of your leadership quality. When you enter politics, even at the local level, you are entering into an arena of war and the battle is especially intense when you challenge the power of the establishment so expect the skirmish. Have confidence that at the end of the day, if you stand strong in the face this type of tyranny you will, de-facto, be standing up for the freedom of all Americans and this will be understood, at least subconsciously, by well-meaning people.

As Henry Ford II famously said in response to a scandal, *never complain, never explain.* (5.) You must stand up in the face of this type of destructive bullying and name-calling and you must unequivocally reject this type of smear in no uncertain terms. Even if they uncover something in your past that you might have said or that you might have written, something that you probably should not have said or written, or if you have to confront something that they might dig up and twist into trying to prove that you have something against another person or another group, you must stand up and reject the usually out of context characterization in clear terms. If they uncover something that really is problematic, own it, disavow it, apologize, and note that you have evolved since then. Then proceed to turn the tables with a pre-planned examination of your opponent's record on the same issue. Know that the sharks will attack if they smell blood. You might also note that if you're on the right side of the establishment, this type of history is more often obscured and ignored as was, for example the segregationist early years of Joe Biden when he was first elected Senator from Delaware in the 1970's.

Indeed, if you prepare in advance for this type of incoming fusillade, if you have done your homework in terms of creating a dossier on yourself, you might be able to turn the situation around to your advantage. If, for example, your opponent tries to smear you as a racist based upon some trivial remark that you might have made years pervious you might be able to turn it around and talk about your opponent's lack of a record, or worse, regarding their involvement in, for example, promoting the development of Black business, employment, education or entrepreneurialism. Have they done anything to improve Black neighborhoods or schools? What is their position on vouchers to young Black students who qualify for charter or private schools? What is their record on reducing crime and drugs in Black neighborhoods? Careful and thoughtful planning in advance, and in anticipation of this type of cynical political attack, might actually offer you an opportunity to present positive proposals to address problems while contrasting those proposals with the empty rhetoric and the non-performance of your opponent.

While you should be prepared to be interviewed by local media once you file papers that establish your intention to run for the office you seek, and by filing such papers with your local town clerk you will be able to begin to raise money, you should also consider hiring a press agent if you have the money. A gook press agent is key to a successful campaign as this person, who should have at least some experience and some proven connections with the local media in your district, would help you to craft messages that might more likely lead to print, radio or TV interviews. Be careful when hiring such a person as there are usually a lot of charlatans who will hover around you hoping to land the gig. If you cannot afford such a person, you might be able to make a deal with a College student majoring in marketing, communications or political science. You might be able to find such a person by placing an ad in your local College newspaper or by placing a notice on a College employment board.

I should emphasize that you should develop a deep and comprehensive knowledge on at least one if not two or three of the issues that you choose to champion and you should be able to articulate that knowledge with an air of authority and under heavy scrutiny. It would be helpful for you to connect some element of your career or activities to your claim of expertise on the issue. Your knowledge should include a philosophy and practical proposals which you should be prepared to present in power point style.

Do not forget that, as a citizen candidate, whether you are on the right or on the left, the media will not be your friend. Reporters are trained to win you over, to gain your confidence and to disarm you as a means to get you to talk and to say things that is either stupid or to say something that they can use against you. Do not be fooled…these people are dangerous! You should never meet with a reporter or go to an editorial board meeting unaccompanied. You should be careful to weigh and measure every word you say in those situations.

For the sake of illustration, I shall present to you 2 scenarios that occurred during my campaign for Congress in Massachusetts. In the first scenarios, I was invited to meet with David S. Bernstein, political reporter for the since defunct and ultra-liberal Boston Phoenix, at the office of the newspaper. I was the conservative Republican candidate for Congress running against liberal icon Barney Frank and, as such, I did not expect a softball interview by any stretch. Bernstein, who pulled no punches, started out with the proverbial "how often do you beat your wife" question. This tactic, which is actually quite common, starts off with a bad assumption, which is presented as an assumed truth, and which immediately puts the candidate on the defensive. It is astonishing to me how often candidates fall into this trap by defending themselves against a false premise.

Bernstein asked me how I, as a right-wing extremist, expected to win an election against such a revered politician as Barney Frank. I countered by politely asking him to please provide me with an example or two that would indicate that I held an extreme position on an issue. Right off the bat, and without saying so, I had rejected his premise and I had turned the tables on him by making him justify his charge. He responded with two charges, one of which was completely false and the other of which was out of context.

On the first charge, where he claimed that I had called for the abolition of the Internal Revenue Service, I responded, somewhat sardonically, by noting that it was not my habit to publicly engage in wishful thinking. While confidently noting that I had never said any such thing, and I knew that I had not and that he had either made this up or he had severely twisted something that I may have written, I turned the tables by noting that no politician could ever get rid of the IRS, that the IRS was here to stay whether we liked it or not, and that such a pronouncement from a politician represented an arrogant overstatement that was all too common.

The second charge that he lobbed at me was that I wanted to abolish public education. I denied this and asked for his evidence. He noted that I was a supporter of home-schooling, implying that such support was a cause of right-wing extremists who wanted to abolish public schools. I charged him with conflating two separate issues, and I followed up with an anecdote about an ultra-liberal couple that I knew, without mentioning any names, who were home-schooling their children with the assertion that home-schooling crossed ideological lines. I followed this up by asking him whether he thought that perhaps many of the liberal readers of the Boston Phoenix, who often think of themselves as anti-establishment, might share some of my concerns over high taxes, intrusive government and big corporate public schools. The Boston Phoenix never ran the interview which tells me that they were not able to get anything on me and, thus, that they would have nothing to say.

The second scenario that I shall raise for the sake of illustration is a lot uglier and was a lot more damaging to me both as a candidate and personally and that was an attempt to prove that I was homophobic, that I had something against gay men and women. Any candidate who fails to genuflect to the will of the establishment should expect defamatory smears of this type to be lodged against them and should expect, given that the establishment controls big media, damage to be done. Right off the bat, I was running against America's first openly gay congressman who was, as such, an establishment cult figure and this was in the year that the Massachusetts Supreme Judicial Court had declared same-sex marriage legal.

I had written hundreds of published columns and these were vigorously scoured by the opposition and, I should note, doing this was fair game. They had uncovered one extremely stupid thing that I had written, and they had run this up the flagpole as evidence that I had something against gay men and women. In this charged atmosphere, I was contacted by a national reporter, who had already interviewed Frank, who wanted to know my thoughts on such questions as same-sex marriage. The reporter had been given a copy of a fundraising letter that my campaign had sent out stating that I was opposed to the "gay agenda" and the reporter wanted clarification on what I had meant by that. In the letter I had defined the gay agenda by raising my opposition to three things, same-sex marriage, ENDA, and hate crimes legislation.

I noted that my position on same-sex marriage was identical to that of former President Bill Clinton, the 2004 Democratic nominee for President John Kerry, and the Democratic Platform, which was that I supported DOMA, the Defense of Marriage Act, which allowed marriage regulation to reside with the states. I opposed ENDA because I believed that it would constitute a national program of affirmative action for gay men and women and would, as such, constitute an extreme incursion by the federal government into the private sector, one that was not, unlike similar laws countering discrimination against African-Americans, warranted by any statistically significant level of discrimination. I opposed hate crimes because such laws would, I argued, criminalize speech and this contradicted the American philosophy of Justice which was based upon action as opposed to opinion or thought however heinous those opinions or thoughts might be.

I tried to turn the tables on Barney Frank who, I should again note, was viewed at the time as a national leader of the gay rights movement. I called him out for not having taken a leadership position during the AIDS crisis, a time when tens of thousands of gay men suffered terrible deaths form this dread disease, including several gay men that I personally knew. I blamed him for placing the interests of the sexual revolution over the lives and the safety of his fellow gay men by not publicly warning gay men about the various homosexual practices that a preponderance of scientists were at the time claiming caused the spread of the disease or by not advocating for sensible public policies during the AIDS pandemic such as at least temporarily shutting down gay bath houses. I expressed the opinion, in an attempt to turn the classic leftist agit-prop tactic to my advantage, that Barney Frank, by his lack of action and by his preference for a political agenda that did not factor in public safety and common sense, had the blood of thousands of gay men on his hands.

Do not expect this type of tactic to necessarily work out for you as, if you are anti-establishment or if you are not on the left side of the political spectrum, this approach was not fashioned for you to employ. Needless to say, I was not able to pull this off.

FREE MEDIA

About a year before I ran for Congress in Massachusetts, 2002-2003, I hosted a half hour per week cable TV show in my community. I would go to the local cable studio once a week where I would interview a guest. Local cable stations offer these programs to any and all residents of a community. All you have to do is go to the office of the local cable station and sign up. You might be required to get some training which they would provide, as I did to get a show at the Boston Neighborhood Network which also charged me a $50 annual membership fee, but most cable stations have easier standards, and most are free.

I soon discovered that my weekly show was re-run at various times of the day and night all during the week. The cable stations do this because they have plenty of open time that they need to fill. I also discovered that I could get other stations in the surrounding communities to carry my show as long as a resident that I knew from each community went over to their local cable office and requested the show in writing by filling out a form. Once this was done, I could drop off a tape of each show to each station. I noticed that after three months of my hosting the show which played regularly on my local cable station, people were starting to recognize me on the street.

I hosted my cable show before the advent of YouTube and social media. Now, with YouTube and with all of the other online video platforms such as Vimeo, Rumble, Minds and Gab, you can set up a free channel where you can download your cable show. YouTube also offers you access to download most videos and you can live stream on

YouTube. This is a great tool for you to reach people directly in your district by asking them to subscribe to your station and by promoting your candidacy with both your YouTube videos and with your live streams. Set up your YouTube channel with a thumbnail photo, some graphics, and a description with links listed in the about section. Having a YouTube station is like having your own TV station and its free.

Social networks provide you with a free means by which you can get your message out to your audience in your own voice and in your own hand. Your message will be your own and, as such, your message will not be tampered with or interpreted or, as it were, misinterpreted by some media outlet. You should set up a free blog on either Blogger or WordPress, both of which are free, where you can write short blogs on various issues and send them around to your social network and the media at large. You should set up a Twitter and a Parlor account specifically for your campaign and you should set up a separate page for your campaign as an addition to your personal Facebook page. You might consider setting up a Tic Tok account where you can record a daily 30 or 60 second commentary and where you can livestream and build an audience.

The keys to success on social media is to operate with consistency as you should commit to recording a certain number of videos and to writing a certain number of blogs each week. I recommend that you record at least 3 videos and that you write at least 3 blogs per week and I recommend that you try to record and post them at the same time of the day on each of the days you create them. You might consider using your blog to maintain an ongoing diary-like record of your campaign. Writing a blog is a great way to clarify your thinking on any given topic and writing requires you to do a bit of a deep dive in terms of research. Do not get hung up on formality as the style today for videos and for blogs is informal and conversational. Just be yourself and speak and write from your heart.

Instagram is a great site for downloading relevant photos and as a means to reach a younger audience. LinkedIn is a great site for linking with professionals who might help you with media, campaigning, support and issue development. You can use Zoom to interview your YouTube guests on a split-screen, guests both in your district and from anywhere else, guests who might help you to gain exposure or guests who might help you to grow your audience by posting the interview on their social network or in other various ways. If you conduct an interview on Zoom, you can simultaneously stream it live onto YouTube while recording it to your desktop to be downloaded into other channels such as Rumble and Minds. Offering an invitation to someone to join you for a talk on YouTube is a great way to meet important people. Most of these services are free, they can be integrated with each other in various ways, and they can be used as platforms to reach more people who might be able to help you and your campaign, or they can simply serve as a means to build followers.

Social networking offers you the opportunity to link with various similar people and groups as well as with other citizen politicians around the country which contributes to an interlocking network of patriots who can offer each other mutual support on a lot of different levels. In these times of censorship from Big Tech, new and alternative social sites are springing up all the time. As this book goes to print, for example, I just discovered and just joined a new one called Brand New Tube.

MONEY

While you may not need much money to run for local office, you should nevertheless register your candidacy with the local equivalent of the Federal Elections Commission, if your state has such a registry for a local office, as a means to formally declare your candidacy. This registration will allow you to accept donations, hold fundraising events and draw media attention. Once you file a document indicating that you intend to run, or once you file a follow-up document that formally declares that you are running, you must proceed to be absolutely exacting, down to the penny, in terms of keeping a record of every amount of money that enters your coffers and who sent it. Study your local laws pertaining to campaign contributions and do not deviate from those laws by one single iota. If you do, particularly as an alternative citizen candidate, I can almost guarantee you that you will be caught and, when you are caught, you will be finished as a candidate and you could end up in big trouble with the law.

You should set up a website that has links to all of your social networks, one that contains a couple of pages presenting your positions on issues, one that has a page linking to media interviews, a contact page, a link for voters to fill out absentee ballots, and a button that links to your campaign bank account for donations. Keep the website simple, clean, easy to navigate, not too wordy, and use primary colors and bold fonts. Creating a campaign website can be done cheaply through WordPress and you can hire a web designer and a WordPress web maintenance person through Fiverr.

A solid way to raise small donations is by asking supporters, local activists, members of your local city or town Republican or Democratic committee to set up coffee for you in their home where you can meet neighbors, deliver a brief informal speech, take questions, schmooze, and raise funds. Do not forget to personally ask every single person in the room to vote for you.

THE CAMPAIGN

First and foremost, the very core activity of your campaign should always be the process, as discussed earlier, of gathering signatures which are required in order to get on the ballot. You should do this personally as much as possible by going door to door or by standing outside of bus-stops and at various events that might take place in your district. You should reach out to all of the local Republican or Democratic city and town committees as well as to local clubs and social organizations in your district requesting that they host an event for you. At such events, you should be prepared to deliver short and pithy remarks, raise funds, gather signatures, ask for votes and recruit volunteers to gather signatures, make phone calls, and conduct activities such as sign-holding and getting out the vote on Election Day.

Fundraising, dependent upon the office that you seek and whether you are able to self-finance, and I should note that if you are able to or if you are willing to self-finance you should report your own donations down to the penny, will determine whether or not you open an office-headquarters and such things as the purchase of signs, buttons, push-cards, advertising, mailers and other effects. I would suggest that less is best and that you first exploit all that is free before spending money. One of the most basic and essential tools of the campaign is the simple push-card or flyer which should have a standard head-shot photo, graphics and fonts that match the campaign website, a short bio, a list of positions with brief descriptions, and contact information. These flyers can be created and printed cheaply, they should be distributed when possible to neighborhood stores, restaurants, backs, groceries, libraries and other locations that might have a bulletin board. Ask a store owner if you can tape a flyer to the window and, with permission, tape the flyer back-to-back with one side facing out and one facing in. Keep a pile of flyers with you at all times to be used as a handout to a potential supporter.

Do a walk-around in a business district accompanied by at least 1 or 2 supporters preferably holding signs. Wave to traffic at intersections. Walk into businesses and diners to introduce yourself, politely and unobtrusively, to the manager. Engage in conversation with the manager and with customers on issues and ask for their vote. For the walk-around it is best to dress somewhat formally. Keep informed on any and all public events in your district and try to make an appearance at as many of these as possible.

You should contact various special interest groups that you resonate with and that might have supporters in your district to ask them for an endorsement. This might involve filling out a questionnaire. Such an endorsement, besides serving as a newsworthy event that could lead to a media interview, could involve what is known as "in-kind" support, which is to say help by volunteers to make phone calls and hold signs and, in rare occasions, such an endorsement might include a donation. Such groups exist on both sides of issues such as abortion and gun control as well as groups such as Chambers of Commerce, the Catholic Church, support for recognizing the Armenian Genocide, the Log Cabin Republicans, NARAL, the NRA and other such groups.

Election Day will most likely be the quietest and the most peaceful day of the campaign. Everything has been done, for better or for worse, and a calm will set in as you sit back and wait for the results and reflect on the experience. You should notify the media in advance of your whereabouts in terms of where and when you and your family will be voting, and they should be given personal contact information so they can reach you with a comment once the results start rolling in. That way they can get a victory or a concession comment when the time arises. You might make a few last-minute phone calls regarding getting supporters to the polls.

You will feel a type of glow of excitement and relief that comes at the conclusion of a prolonged and hard-fought fight. All will be in the hands of the voters.

GOING FORWARD

I shall conclude this short treatise with positive but not pollyannaish words of encouragement. The trend in America today is, I believe, one that is moving us in the direction toward a re-assertion of local democratic control over our political life and destiny. Such an assertion of control, by means of patriotic citizen politicians running for and assuming local offices, will interrupt and will erode the powers of the entrenched oligarchies both on the state and on the national level and will, over time, overtake those usurped powers. The movement that Donald Trump launched has triggered a drive toward a return of sovereignty to its rightful owner, the people under God, as this movement has caused a rejection, on a mass scale, of the power of the corrupt and imperialistic globalist corporatist elite establishment.

The massively growing citizen juggernaut will be sustained by a developing consciousness and, as a result, by an emerging conscience and a certain resolve on the part of the average working citizen who will increasingly become a citizen activist and a citizen politician. This growing consciousness which, I should note, is developing rapidly worldwide, is based upon an awareness of a political theory of government that was embraced by the founding generation of Americans, a theory which holds, as stated by the Declaration of Independence, that: *we are endowed by our creator with certain inalienable rights, that among these are life, liberty and the pursuit of happiness.*

We as a people are becoming aware, in a nutshell, that in the context of the limited sovereignty that we as individuals possess, we are nevertheless in control over our own lives and over our own destinies to the degree that we are willing to step up and fight for that control. We are waking up to our own power. We are becoming aware of the fact that we derive our limited sovereignty, and as human beings we are naturally limited and, as such, we are not God but, rather, we are imperfect images of God, from Almighty God who is the great sovereign, who is the source of all creation and who is the giver of the law.

Thomas Jefferson clearly articulated this foundational principle when he noted that we the people are endowed by the Creator with inalienable rights and, by implication, that we are not endowed by the man-made state. At the end of the day, we are answerable to God, or as Jefferson expressed this, we are answerable to nature and to natures God, and not to the earthly power of the State. This concept was articulated by Jesus when he answered the mighty Roman Governor Pontius Pilate, who represented the corrupt elite powers of his time, by declaring that he answered not to the Roman Empire but to a higher authority. Jesus was crucified within hours of taking this courageous stand and his example has inspired freedom-oriented people and movements ever since.

This philosophical principle stands as the governing idea of the American Republic and this is true whether or not one believes in a divine creator. John Adams articulated this principle when he noted that ours is a government of laws and not of men by which he recognized that natural law is based upon abstract truths and not man-made laws. The American founding generation stood up against an enemy that sought to usurp those natural rights, which are based upon abstract truths, by fighting a six-year war of independence and by establishing the principle of self-government. Every generation since has had to stand up against the corrupting encroachments of an elite that seeks, often by crafty and subversive means, to create laws out of whole cloth and, as such, that seeks to abuse power as a means to suit their agendas and to advance their artificial and arbitrary whim.

As Americans, we are rapidly waking up to the fact that the best, the least corrupt, the most effective and the most natural form of government is local government. We are growing increasingly aware of the fact that local government has been effectively gutted over time by a growing national and even an international unelected interlocking power structure. We are becoming aware of the degree by which our local governments have sold out their sovereign function by accepting benefits and gifts from bigger government structures that are interlocked with private interests, all of which attach strings to those gifts and those benefits. Such arrangement have led, over time and almost imperceptibly, to a transfer of governing powers from the local elected official, elected by the local community to represent the unique interests of the electorate, to a web of permanent, unelected, faceless and in many cases mechanized bureaucracies. Those unelected bureaucracies now wield governing and, as such, decision making powers over increasing aspects of our lives, our economies, our businesses, our education, our health, our families, our property, our means of communication and our overall welfare.

The job of the citizen politician is to demand a return of those powers to the rightful owner, the people, whose will and interests are properly expressed by those who they elect to represent their interests in local government. Thus, for example, the local elected citizen school board member, having discovered that the school board has little if any actual say over the curriculum of the public school, or little to say about much of anything else that is going in the school district and who, as such, only holds power over cosmetic and trivial functions, must demand that those governing powers be returned to their rightful democratic loci which is the elected school board. The elected citizen school board member must go into the schools, must examine and expose the curriculum in all of its aspects, must open the process to public scrutiny, must hold hearings, question contracts and demand changes when warranted.

I can assure you that this process, this challenge to entrenched power, will not be easy and that this type of challenge with take an incredible amount of fortitude and a strong stomach. No one shoves a stick into a beehive without getting a couple of stings. Yet, the elected citizen politician will find that they are not alone in the battle as growing cadres of citizens, from all sides of the political spectrum, will step up and go to bat for the courageous citizen once the establishment launches its inevitable campaign of calumny and destruction. The courageous citizen politician will be gratified to witness how many of his or her neighbors will be willing to join him in the breach. The courageous citizen politician will know that he or she is striking a blow for freedom and truth and he will know with a sense of certainty that he is making a difference. The citizen politician, as a human being, will sleep more soundly at night and will experience a sense of inner peace knowing that he is on the right side of history.

NOTES

1. Adams, Henry, *The Education f Henry Adams,* Wilder Publications, 2009, first published 1918
2. Mass Moments, a project of Mass. Humanities, Tip O'Neill Announces Run for Congress, April 16, 1952
3. Matthews, Chris, *Hardball: How Politics is Played, told by one who knows the Game,* Simon & Schuster, 1999
4. Besancon, Alain, *The Falsification of the Good: Soloviev and Orwell,* Claridge Press LTD, 1994

5. Lasky, Victor, *Never Complain, Never Explain: The Story of Henry Ford II*, R. Marek Publishers, 1981

www.ingramcontent.com/pod-product-compliance
Lightning Source LLC
Chambersburg PA
CBHW072328270726
48658CB00016B/2126